ACTION MODEL BOOK

COLUMBUS REACHES AMERICA

Written by David Marshall

PICCOLO

COLUMBUS REACHES AMERICA

Written by David Marshall

Conceived and produced by
Bender Richardson White
PO BOX 266
Uxbridge UB9 5NX
England

Editor: Lionel Bender
assisted by Madeleine Samuel
Designer: Ben White
Production: Kim Richardson
Media conversion: Peter MacDonald and
Partners
Illustrator: Peter Dennis
Model Artwork: Hayward Art Group

First published in Great Britain in 1991
by Pan Macmillan Children's Books
a division of Pan Macmillan Ltd
18-21 Cavaye Place
London SW10 9PG

Printed in Spain

ISBN 0-330-31628-1

A CIP catalogue record of this book is
available from the British Library

INTRODUCTION

Five hundred years ago, in 1492, explorer Christopher Columbus set sail westward from Spain into unknown waters. After a voyage lasting more than two months, he reached land. He had 'discovered' the Americas. He was the first European to set foot in what was to become known as the New World.

Columbus Reaches America commemorates that great event in two interesting and exciting ways. The first is a book-to-keep, a 32-page illustrated reference book that explains the history, geography and politics associated with Columbus's great voyages to the Americas. The second is a model-to-make, a cut out and glue card model of the *Niña*, one of Columbus's great ships along with the *Santa Maria* and the *Pinta*.

The book traces why Columbus wanted to voyage west, how he raised the money to do so, and what he found when he reached America. It also describes what daily life was like on board his ships, the historical importance of his voyages and, in the years that followed, how other European explorers such as Drake, Magellan, Cortes and Pizarro opened up the Americas. The model, in scale detail, reproduces the beauty and fragility of Columbus's ships. You can use the model both in connection with the book and as a display item on your desk or window-ledge. Instructions for removing the centre card section and building the model are given on pages 16 and 17 of the book.

We hope you enjoy **Columbus Reaches America**

CONTENTS

500 YEARS AGO

'Tierra! Tierra!' – the cry that land has been sighted. Certainly the most welcome sound for any mariner who sailed off into the unknown. It is impossible for us to imagine what it must have been like for members of Columbus's crew on 12 October 1492 to hear that cry. It was over 30 days since they had seen land. They had no idea where they were, or where they were going. All they were aware of was the seemingly never-ending sea.

Then, suddenly, 'Land! Land!' The excitement on the ships was a mixture of relief, happiness, triumph and thanks to God. The noise must have been amazing! Columbus christened the first island he set foot on, San Salvador – Spanish for 'the Saviour'. This certainly proves the great relief it must have been, and shows his gratitude to God for delivering him safely into the 'Indies'.

◁ One of the hardest, but most important, jobs on board ship was that of the lookout. Perched up on top of the main mast, it was uncomfortable and lonely. If the crew were restless about finding land the lookout was constantly under scrutiny from the decks. The lookout on Columbus's second ship, the *Pinta*, Rodrigo de Triana, never really got the recognition he deserved. But no lookout in history can have made a more welcome or momentous sighting of land.

1992 Commemorative Events In 1992 the focus of the whole world is going to be on Spain. Firstly, the importance of Columbus's first voyage to the Americas from Spain 500 years earlier will be remembered in many ways. One of these is to be the reconstruction of Columbus's sailing ships and a repeat of his first voyage from Palos to the islands of the Caribbean. Secondly, the World Fair for all major industrial nations will this time take place in Spain. This biannual event will be held in Seville, in southern Spain, and will be called Expo '92. Thirdly, one of the two most important sporting events in the world is to be held in Barcelona in 1992 – the Olympic Games. Fourthly, the European City of Culture in 1992 is Barcelona.

Where did Columbus land?

Even today there is uncertainty over exactly where Columbus landed. In 1922 Watling Island was renamed San Salvador, as most people thought then that it was where Columbus arrived. However, investigators and historians who have been trying since to establish with certainty just where he first set foot in the 'New World', now believe it was more likely to have been the island of Samana Cay.

One thing Columbus himself was absolutely certain of in 1492 was that he had achieved an amazing feat. He was sure that he had reached 'the Indies'. That is why he called the first natives he met Indians, and why today the islands are known as the West Indies.

Driven by a burning ambition

Everyone is agreed both then and since that Columbus's journeys were outstandingly important. He made possible later voyages and discoveries, and set a date in history that provides a turning point. All his life Columbus had a vision and a belief that he had been given a destiny by God. He pursued his idea fanatically and everything that happened seemed to confirm his belief. It is not surprising, then, that 1992 will see some amazing events to commemorate his voyage.

▽ **Success – by the will of God**
The following is a translation of a prayer that Columbus said on landing on San Salvador as he realised he had opened up the rest of the world:
"O Lord, Almighty and Everlasting God, by Thy Holy Word Thou hast created the heaven, and the Earth, and the sea; blessed and glorified be Thy Name, and praised be Thy Majesty, which hath designed to use us, Thy humble servants, that Thy Holy Name may be known and proclaimed in this second part of the Earth."

Here Columbus is shown meeting natives of San Salvador.

COLUMBUS THE EXPLORER

◁ No actual drawings or paintings of Columbus exist. We do have pen-portraits of him though. He is described as: *"A well-built man of more than average height. His face is long with rather high cheek bones; his person neither fat nor thin. He has a hooked nose, light eyes and a fair skin with a ruddy tinge."*

COLOMBVS

Christopher Columbus was born in 1451, in Genoa, Italy. (Amerigo Vespucci, an explorer who because of his name almost betters Columbus's place in history, was also born in Italy in 1451.) While at school he was sent by his father on a trading voyage. It was then he decided he wanted to be a famous seaman. He learnt maths and geometry, astronomy, mapmaking, and Latin. This last subject was essential as it meant he could read all the books he needed on astronomy. When he felt he knew enough, he left the family weaving business and went to sea. Between 1465 and 1476 Columbus, the Genoese mariner, visited many foreign places conducting trade wherever he went. For instance, he went on a Portuguese ship on a trip from Lisbon to the Azores, and on to Ireland and Iceland. In 1476 Columbus moved with his family to Portugal. In late 1478 he married the daughter of a Portuguese nobleman. This gave him the money to carry on trading. When on his journeys to the Gold Coast of Africa he learnt how important it was to have beads and trinkets to trade. It was during these travels that he heard from other traders of the fabulous wealth of India and China. He realised that any captain who could sail west to Asia would gain undreamed of riches.
Columbus learnt a great deal about the size and shape of the

THE UNKNOWN
Explorers in the 15th century were often terrified by the fantastic tales of early travellers. They saw pictures and read descriptions of headless men with faces on their chest, dog-faced men with blue hairy bodies, shadowfeet people who used their own large feet as sunshades, and people who slept in the shelter of their own huge ears!

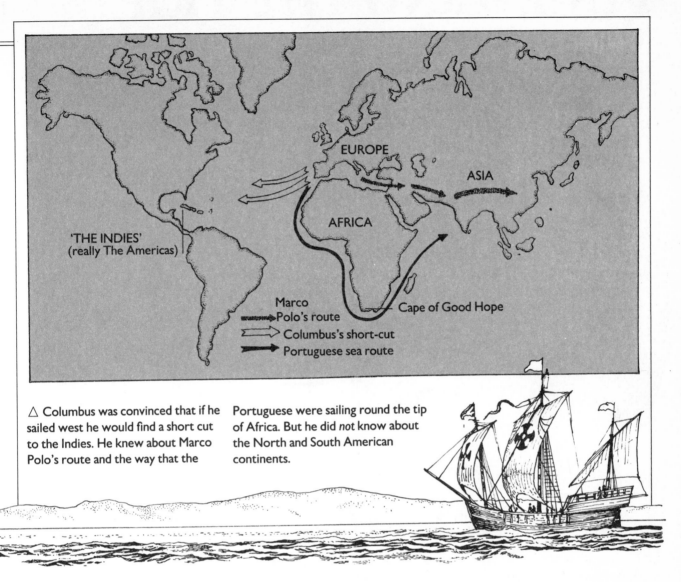

△ Columbus was convinced that if he sailed west he would find a short cut to the Indies. He knew about Marco Polo's route and the way that the Portuguese were sailing round the tip of Africa. But he did *not* know about the North and South American continents.

world, and the excitement of exploring, from reading the book of the 13th-century travels of Marco Polo in China. A copy of the book has been found with notes in the margins written by Columbus – particulary the chapters on India and China. This is why he became obsessed with the idea of reaching the 'Indies' by going west. He was convinced that crossing the 'Ocean Sea' (the Atlantic Ocean) would be a short-cut to Cipangu (Japan), and the gold he wanted.

In 1476 there was still an argument about whether the world was flat or round. Most educated people knew that the Earth was round but no-one knew how big it was. Marco Polo wrote that Cipangu (Japan) was about 3000km east of China. From this Columbus decided that Japan was 5000km west of Europe. In fact it is nearly 18,000km. There was one other problem too. Mapmakers of the time only included three continents in their maps – Europe, Asia and Africa. They had no idea that in the westward direction the continents of North and South America were between Europe and China. This was to make it impossible for Columbus to achieve what he believed was his destiny – to cross the Ocean Sea and take God's words to people in the East.

Columbus wrote out a version of this part of 1st century Roman philosopher Seneca's *Medea*, in Latin. His conceited nature meant that he thought it applied to him:

"There will come a time in the long years of the world when the Ocean Sea will loosen its shackles and a great part of the Earth will be opened up and a new sailor such as Jason's guide, shall discover a new world – and then shall Thule (northern Europe) no longer be the last of lands."

FINANCING THE TRIP

Columbus had to persuade wealthy people to give or lend him the necessary money for his voyage to the Indies. In 1484 he presented his plans to King John II of Portugal. The King called up a special commission of experts to examine the plan. Without Columbus knowing, the commission sent out a ship of its own to follow his planned route. It came back with reports of nothing but endless sea. Inevitably the King refused to finance Columbus's scheme. In disgust Columbus moved to Spain.

He presented his plans to Isabella and Ferdinand, Queen and King of Spain, in May 1486. The Queen, too, set up a commission of experts to examine his plans. Columbus was encouraged because Isabella obviously liked his ideas and gave him a small income to live on while she waited for the report. It seemed to take forever.

▽ In 1488 Columbus sent his plans back to the King of Portugal. Before Columbus could argue for the plans, the Portuguese-sponsored explorer Bartholomew Diaz returned from reaching the Cape of Good Hope at the tip of Africa and opening up the Indian Ocean. King John didn't need Columbus anymore, and said so!

DIAZ RETURNS TO GENOA – COLUMBUS REJECTED

Columbus sent his brother to argue his case with King Henry VII of England. He wasn't interested. Neither was the King of France. At last the commission of experts in Spain presented its report to Ferdinand and Isabella. They too thought the plan an impossibility! Isabella, however, was not convinced that the experts were right, and asked Columbus to wait and present his plans after their war with the Kingdom of Granada in Spain was over. By January 1492 the war had ended and Columbus went to explain his plan. The King and Queen could hardly believe their ears as Columbus made extravagant demands about how he was to be honoured and rewarded for taking on such an adventure. They refused to finance the trip.

Columbus set off once more to try to convince the King of France. It must have been an incredible moment when Columbus, already on the road, was overtaken by a messenger and told that Queen Isabella wanted him to return to the court. They would agree to ALL his demands after all. He had got his money. He was on his way at last!

▽ Their majesties, King Ferdinand and Queen Isabella of Spain, were excited by the possibility of trading with the fabulously rich Chinese and listened carefully to Columbus's plans.

COLUMBUS AT ISABELLA'S COURT

SETTING SAIL

On Friday, 3 August 1492, Columbus set sail from Palos in southern Spain on his first voyage into unexplored waters. He believed that his destination, Cipangu (Japan), lay due west of the Spanish-occupied Canary Islands. So the fleet at first headed south-west hoping to pick up easterly winds. Three days out of port the rudder cable of the *Pinta* snapped and the ship leaked badly. Martin Pinzon, the captain of the *Pinta*, was convinced that it had been cut deliberately. The fear of the unknown for some of the crew had been too much. Columbus made an unplanned stop at the Canaries for repairs. While in harbour, he also took on fresh supplies and changed the *Niña*'s sails. The fleet sailed again on 6 September.

A little deceit went a long way
Columbus was only too aware of the fear of his sailors. So that they would not expect to reach land earlier than was likely,

Stores on board the *Santa Maria*
18 tonnes of wheat, 2 tonnes of flour, 8 tonnes of dry biscuits.
17 tonnes of wine in barrels.
1 tonne of rum, 1 tonne of whisky.
1 tonne of cheese, 1 tonne of salt pork.
Dried fish, beans, lentils, figs, almonds, rice, salt, pepper, vinegar, olive oil, honey, garlic.
Medicines and fresh water.
Pigs, hens (killed at sea).
Tools, planks, pitch, tar, fat, sulphur, cooking pots and pans, knives, candles, lamps, oil.
Sailcloth, leather, ropes, tackle, blocks, flags, anchors, buoys.
Crossbows, arrows, helmets, shields, swords, muskets, cannons.
Navigational instruments, clocks, maps, writing materials.
Prayer books.
Gold, silver, spices (for trading).

The Crews
Sailors and officers.
Government officials.
Surgeons and priests.
Locksmiths, crossbowmen.
Farmers.
Cooks and assistants.
Ship's boys.

The Fleet

Columbus was in command of three, well-stocked ships. They were his flagship, the *Santa Maria*, and the much smaller *Pinta* and *Niña*. He led the fleet from the *Santa Maria*, shown below, which was about 25m long and 9m wide. It was built as a trading ship so could carry lots of cargo. The *Pinta* was slightly smaller than the *Santa Maria* but could sail faster. The fleet could make 120km in a day.

Below is a cut-away of the *Santa Maria*. Like all of columbus's ships, it was built from thick oak hull planking fastened with wooden pegs and iron bolts.

Columbus kept two logs each day. One was a true record of the distance they had travelled, the other a false one to deceive the crew. This second one underestimated the distance travelled everyday. If they sailed 60 kilometres, Columbus wrote 48. He showed the crews only the false record and they were fooled. Just because he was inspired by God on his journey did not mean he had to tell the truth! Nonetheless, in their fear and eagerness, the sailors often made false calls of Tierra! Tierra!

▷ The *Niña* was originally fitted with triangular sails but in strong winds these were difficult to control. When the fleet stopped at the Canaries, new masts and square sails were fitted, as shown here.

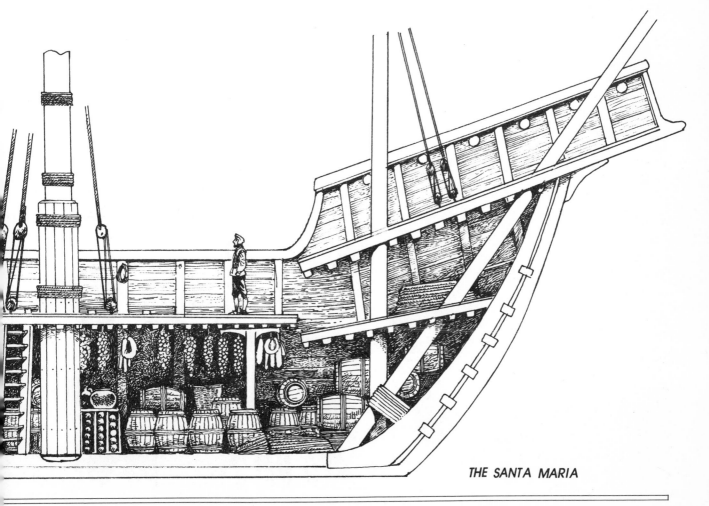

THE SANTA MARIA

OUT AT SEA

Cross-staff

This simple device, shown below, was often used instead of an astrolabe (see opposite) to find the latitude. One straight piece of wood had another cross-piece that ran along it. The cross-piece was lined up with the Sun and the horizon to measure the Sun's altitude in the sky.

The incident with the *Pinta* showed that Columbus's crew were not as convinced as he was about the wisdom of their journey. Many of them had joined the trip to escape from prison. Others had been ordered to go by the Spanish King and Queen. They had no idea what a long sea journey would be like. They were constantly frightened. They were the uneducated people who still thought that the world was flat and the longer they were at sea, and the further they sailed, the nearer they were getting to the edge! Anytime they could fall off!

The crew became more and more restless. On 21 September the wind dropped away completely and the ships were becalmed. What was worse was that the sea was completely covered in weed. After three days, the breeze got up but it was not even strong enough to drive the ships through the weed. The men were convinced they would die. They called the area Sargaco, 'sea plants'. To this day this area is called the Sargasso Sea. If this wasn't bad enough, once the ships were under way again and had been making good progress for a few days, Martin Pinzon on the *Pinta* realised the lies that Columbus had been writing in the log – and said so!

Eventually Columbus convinced Pinzon otherwise, but the men were even more worried than before.

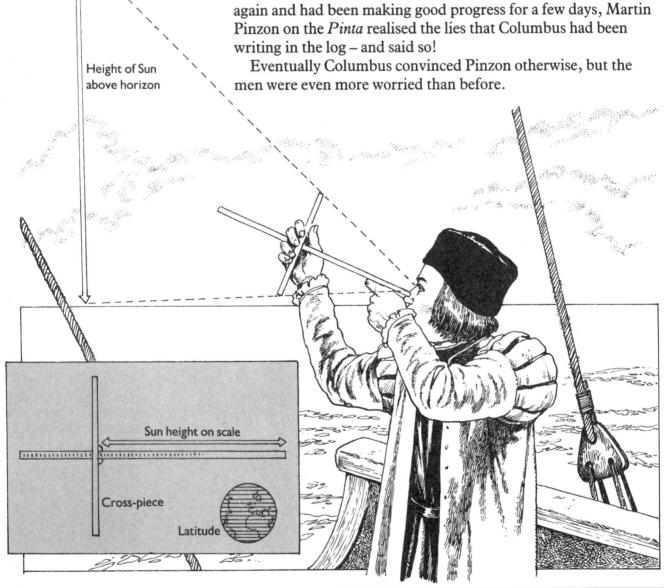

Height of Sun above horizon

Sun height on scale

Cross-piece

Latitude

On 10 October the problem came to a head. The crews were at the point of open mutiny. They had been at sea for 40 days without any sight of land. In desperation Columbus agreed that if they didn't sight land within three days, they would return home. He really did put his trust in God.

NAVIGATING

To find and stay on course, Columbus relied on the simple navigational aids of the time – a mariner's compass, an hour-glass, sea charts, a ruler, a quadrant, an astrolabe, a pair of dividers, a simple multiplication table and a lead plumbline. The compass gave Columbus the direction he was sailing. He would work out the daily distance by multiplying the hours spent on each course by the speed of the ship. The speed of the ship was worked out by watching bubbles or bits of seaweed floating by. On leaving the coast, Columbus took compass bearings of some tall landmarks, estimated the distance from the ship, and then made a mark in his sea chart at the point he thought the ship was. The next day he plotted the course in the same way from this mark, and so on for the rest of his voyage. This way of marking the course is known as dead reckoning. Columbus was extremely good at it.

Astrolabe
Used to measure latitude. A solid metal ring, usually bronze, is marked with the degrees of latitude. A movable arm, fixed in the centre, has sights on each end. The arm is moved round slowly until the Pole Star is lined up by both sights. The point on the ring where the arm cuts the scale on the edge is the latitude.

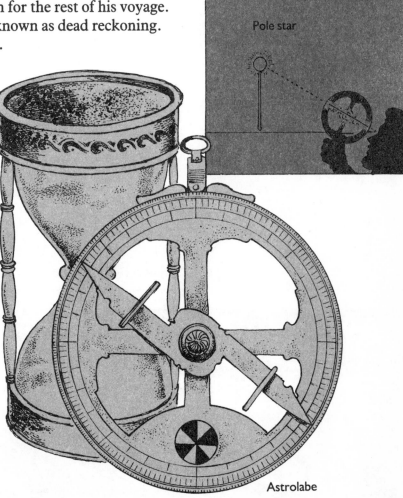

Pole star

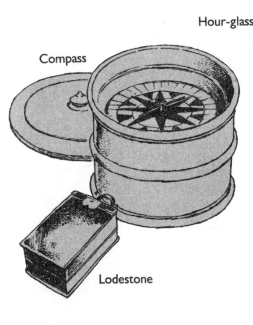

Compass

Hour-glass

Lodestone

Astrolabe

△ Like modern compasses, Columbus's model had a magnetic needle which when mounted on a point always pointed north. A card was fixed underneath the needle with all the points of the compass filled in. An hour-glass, or sand glass, like an egg timer was used to measure the passing of time.

A DAY IN THE LIFE

There are no plans or records left today of the *Santa Maria*, *Pinta* or *Niña*. However, Columbus's letters and books, and documents from other 15th-century sailing ships, make it possible to imagine the daily routine of the crews.

The sailors were divided into two work groups. One group would be on duty, the other off. Work periods, called watches, lasted four hours. During each watch, a boy in charge of the hour-glass called out the time as he reversed the glass. He also called out "All hands on deck!" when it was time for the watches to change over.

Columbus, his captains, royal officials and the officers probably had cabins or sleeping quarters, but the ordinary seamen and marines slept out on the decks. None of them would want to be on the levels below where the smell from the stores would be awful and only rats and cockroaches thrived.

Officers and able seamen at work

From time to time, the officers took navigational measurements and checked the condition and quantities of the stores below decks. To check that the ship was not sailing in waters too shallow, they used a plumbline. This was just a piece of lead on the end of a long rope that they dropped to the bottom of the

1 CALLING THE NEW WATCH

2 MEN AWOKEN FROM SLEEP ON DECK

5 SETTING NEW SAILS AS WINDS PICK UP

6 CHECKING STORES

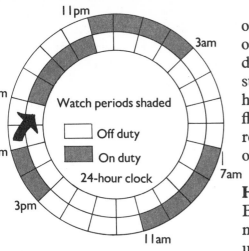

Watch periods shaded

☐ Off duty

■ On duty

24-hour clock

11pm
3am
7am
11am
3pm

Duty periods, or watches, lasted
4 hours, except in the late afternoon,
when there were two 2-hour watches.
By using these short 'dogged watches'
the sailors did not have to work the
same hours each day.

ocean to gauge its depth. If supplies of any foods were running
out, the officers would instruct the cook to change the crew's
diet or to reduce the amounts given to each person so that
supplies would last that much longer. Any crew member late for
his watch or being lazy was punished by the marshall, by
flogging or ducking in the sea. When off-duty, crew members
rested or slept, washed, mended their clothes or bedding, swam,
or sat around playing games or talking to one another.

Hearty meals for all

Each ship had its own cook and assistant, who prepared two
meals a day for the officers, marines and sailors. Breakfast
usually consisted of cheese, fruit, sardines and dry biscuits. The
evening meal, served hot, included beans or peas and a cooked
meat, such as pork or chicken. Food was cooked or heated on
deck in a special iron stove where flames would blow away from
the wooden ship. A bucket of seawater was kept close at hand to
douse any sparks. Live animals were kept on board to be killed
when their meat was required. At the beginning of the voyage,
fresh water was available to drink, but once this had gone stale,
only wine was available. There were no toilets on the ships, so
the crew used buckets which were emptied over the sides.

3 MORNING PRAYERS

4 SCRUBBING THE DECKS WITH A FLAT STONE

7 KEEPING A LOOKOUT FROM THE MASTHEAD

8 COOKING AND EATING SUPPER ON DECK

MAKE YOUR OWN *NIÑA*

What you need
Scissors
Craft knife
Pencil
Ruler
Glue
Biro
Double-sided tape

Firstly, remove the card section from the book. With a knife or a blade of the scissors, lift up the arms of the staples holding the section in place. Then with a sharp tug pull out the section. Fold back the arms of the staples.

1. Cut out all the parts using sharp scissors and gently score along the fold lines for the tabs with a craft knife. Be sure to cut out the holes in the base.

2. Cut slots in the deck for the masts using the craft knife, then push a pencil through the holes to make them neatly round. (See detailed drawings below).

3. Cut a slit for the rudder in the stern (back) of the ship.

4. Fold up the deck, making sure that the angle at A is a right angle (90°).

5. Fold down the flaps along the edges of the deck then glue one side of the deck to either the left or right side of the ship. The deck should be positioned about 1cm below the top edge of the side of the ship. Hold the deck and side together until the glue sets.

This stage and the next are a little fiddly, but its important to ensure the sides of the ship are sufficiently bent round and stuck firmly to the deck at front and back.

6. Stick on the stern section, aligning it at the top with the side panel. Make sure this is firmly in place.

7. Stick on the other side of the ship, again holding it in place until the glue sets.

8. Glue the hull to the seascape base. Adjust the position of the ship and hold it firmly in place until the glue sets by sticking your fingers up through the holes cut in the base.

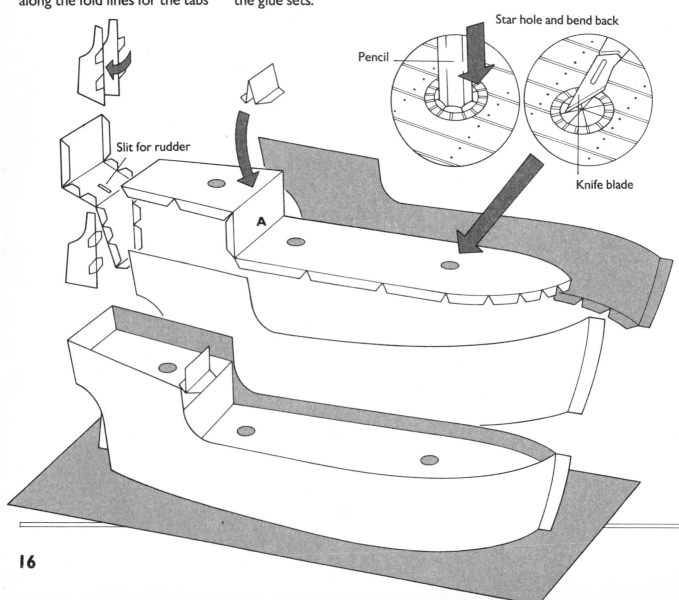

Star hole and bend back

Pencil

Slit for rudder

Knife blade

A

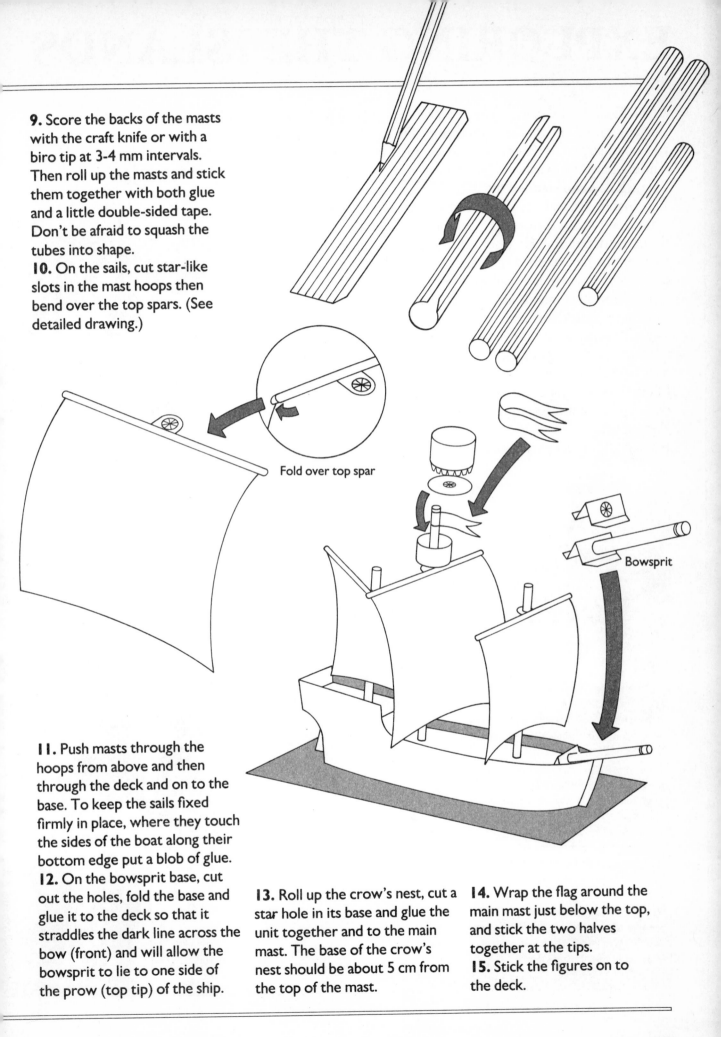

9. Score the backs of the masts with the craft knife or with a biro tip at 3-4 mm intervals. Then roll up the masts and stick them together with both glue and a little double-sided tape. Don't be afraid to squash the tubes into shape.

10. On the sails, cut star-like slots in the mast hoops then bend over the top spars. (See detailed drawing.)

Fold over top spar

Bowsprit

11. Push masts through the hoops from above and then through the deck and on to the base. To keep the sails fixed firmly in place, where they touch the sides of the boat along their bottom edge put a blob of glue.

12. On the bowsprit base, cut out the holes, fold the base and glue it to the deck so that it straddles the dark line across the bow (front) and will allow the bowsprit to lie to one side of the prow (top tip) of the ship.

13. Roll up the crow's nest, cut a star hole in its base and glue the unit together and to the main mast. The base of the crow's nest should be about 5 cm from the top of the mast.

14. Wrap the flag around the main mast just below the top, and stick the two halves together at the tips.

15. Stick the figures on to the deck.

EXPLORING THE ISLANDS

At 2 o'clock in the morning of 12 October, Rodrigo de Triana, the lookout on the *Pinta*, sighted land. On this occasion there was no mistake. At dawn, the fleet set anchor in a bay and a landing party went ashore. Once on land, Columbus raised the Spanish flag and claimed the island for Queen Isabella and King Ferdinand. He was convinced that he had reached an island near China, but this was not Cipangu, the land with the gold and riches he hoped for. He resolved to sail on and look further. He was sure he had reached the edge of the Indies in the East but he didn't know whether to sail west or south to reach Cipangu, Cathay and the Great Khan – and the gold.

Taking six Indians with him as guides, he decided to sail south. It is interesting to note that if he had sailed west, he would have reached Florida, on the mainland of America. He left San Salvador on 14 October 1492 and after sailing for 50 kilometres, he reached a small island that he called Santa Maria de la Concepción. Looping round a long island which he called Fernandina, he reached another small island which he named Isabella. This last part of the journey was about 110 kilometres.

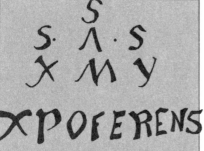

Columbus's signature
on his writings

Columbus's description on first meeting the Indians:
"The men wore very few clothes. The women were the same, although I saw only one. All the people I saw were under 30 years of age. They were well built with handsome bodies and very good faces ... their hair goes down to their eyebrows except for a crop at the back which they never cut. When I showed them a sword they got hold of it by the blade and cut themselves because they did not know what it was. They should be good servants because they soon repeated anything we said to them. I think it will be easy to turn them into Christians because they don't have any religion."

Everywhere he landed, Columbus traded his trinkets for any gold the natives had.

However, sailors on the *Pinta* had become impatient with Columbus and his failure to find the riches they all longed for. So under Martin Pinzon, they struck off on their own. Columbus was furious, but unable to prevent it.

Cipangu or Cuba?

Whilst on Isabella, Columbus heard from the natives of a place called Colba (Cuba) which sounded as though it might be the mainland and have the gold he was seeking. So he left Isabella and sailed south again for about 180 kilometres. On reaching Cuba, Columbus was confused again. This land was big enough to be the mainland but it was nothing like the Indies he had expected to find. So he sent a number of men inland and sailed on to another large island that he called Hispaniola (Española).

After so many days travelling around the islands – over 90 in all – Columbus decided that it was time to return home. The overwhelming reason for this, though, was that the *Santa Maria* had run aground on a coral reef and he only had one ship left – the *Niña*. He might not have achieved all he set out for, but he was convinced that the voyage had been a success, and he had to make sure the people in Spain knew about it!

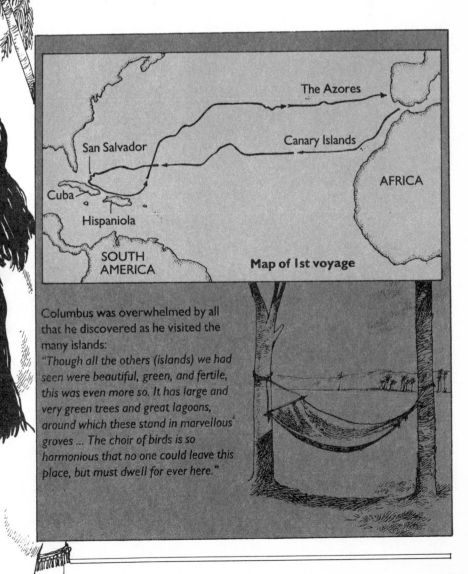

Map of 1st voyage

Columbus was overwhelmed by all that he discovered as he visited the many islands:

"Though all the others (islands) we had seen were beautiful, green, and fertile, this was even more so. It has large and very green trees and great lagoons, around which these stand in marvellous groves ... The choir of birds is so harmonious that no one could leave this place, but must dwell for ever here."

THE WANDERER RETURNS

Before returning home, Columbus had to take all the supplies from the wrecked *Santa Maria* on to the *Niña*, or on to the mainland. Not all the crew could return in the one small ship left, so they used the timber from the wreck to build a fort on Hispaniola and settled here. When it was finished Columbus named the fort *La Navidad* (Christmas).

At the beginning of January 1493 Columbus left *La Navidad* with some of his men to begin the journey home. Two days later he was surprised to see the *Pinta* sailing towards him. With some relief, and concealed anger, Columbus welcomed Martin Pinzon and they sailed back to Hispaniola together. Pinzon gave all sorts of excuses to Columbus for the action he had taken. On 16 January the *Niña* and the *Pinta* left Hispaniola for Spain.

Arms of Columbus as given to him by King Ferdinand and Queen Isabella.

◁ The voyage home proved to be disastrous. Both the *Pinta* and *Niña* were leaking badly, the sailors were tired and longed for home, and then the weather turned to violent storms. It was at this point that the ships got separated again. One moment Columbus looked across and saw the *Pinta* being tossed on the huge waves. The next minute it was gone. Columbus had to sail on alone. Both captains were convinced that the other's ship had capsized.

Columbus was desperate. What if his ship should go down or he die and no-one would know of his achievements? He wrote two brief descriptions of his whole voyage. One he threw overboard in a barrel in the hope it would reach land. The other he fastened to the front of the ship so that it would float away if the ship capsized. Columbus battled on hardly able to cope with the thought that after all he had been through, and the way that Pinzon had disobeyed his orders, he might after all get back to Spain with his amazing news after the *Pinta*. So with even more determination he ordered one small sail slung low on the main mast to be raised, and a permanent watch in the lookout to yell out instructions to the helmsman. This incredible seamanship brought Columbus home safely to Palos – but not before reaching land in the Azores. These islands were owned by the Portuguese. However, the *Niña* was badly damaged and he had no choice but to land. Worse was to follow! On leaving the Azores the storms got even fiercer and Columbus was blown straight into the mainland of Portugal. On 4 March he had to land there. King John immediately demanded to see him. Columbus was in some danger. However, once King John was convinced that Columbus had not been exploring Africa he was free to carry on to Spain.

After an incredible journey Columbus landed safely at Palos on the morning of 15 March 1493. Even more incredibly, Martin Pinzon, in the *Pinta*, after a terrifying journey that took him north to France, reached Palos a few hours later on exactly the same day as Columbus!

Treaty of Tordesillas
Remembering the trouble Columbus had with the Portuguese, it must have been a great relief to him when they reached an agreement with the Spanish over future conquests. The Treaty of Tordesillas was signed by both sides on 7 June 1494. It was agreed that a dividing line would be drawn from north to south about 1700km west of Cape Verde Islands off the coast of West Africa. One result of this today is that Spanish is the native language of all the countries in South America except Brazil which is on the other side of the treaty line, and where Portuguese is the language!

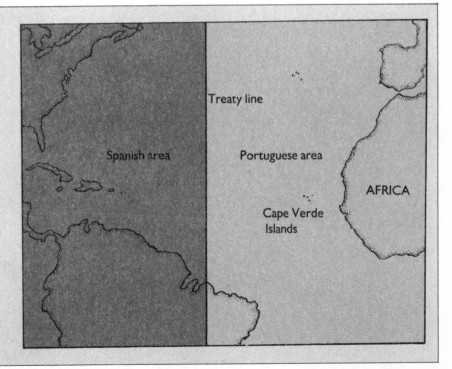

THE SECOND VOYAGE

Columbus was now a rich and famous man. The King and Queen bestowed on him great riches as he explained all that he had discovered. The journey he made through Spain to Barcelona to talk to Ferdinand and Isabella was a triumphal procession. People flocked to see this most famous explorer. The King and Queen were anxious to reward the sailor who had first sighted land. Even though it certainly wasn't Columbus, he accepted this reward himself. He was out for any recompense he could acquire for the risks he had taken, even if it meant depriving someone else. The slightly late and disgraced Martin Pinzon received no rewards at all. He died only a few days later.

From good to bad to worse

After all these accolades, and with his ambition to explore undiminished, it is not surprising that on 25 September 1493 Columbus set sail on his second voyage to the Indies. He called in at the Canaries and then sailed on to the 'East'. Unlike the first journey he decided to take the advice of Indians he had captured and sail west and further south. It worked. Thanks to fine weather and good winds the remaining part of the journey took only three weeks. On 3 November he landed on an island which he called Dominica. This time he had had no reason to lie

Strange discoveries
Columbus hated what he discovered on Dominica. He found the natives eating human flesh, and they had many prisoners waiting to be eaten! He rescued some captives from these natives, who were known as Caribs. The area is the Caribbean today. Although he didn't find the great wealth he desired, he was amazed by some of the things he collected — parrots, iguanas, pineapples, maize, and sweet potatoes. The men on Cuba did not find any gold either, but they did report on the natives who rolled up the dried leaves of plants and sucked in the smoke when they had set them alight. Columbus had discovered cigarettes!

Ferdinand and Isabella gave Columbus three orders:
Take Christianity to the natives; establish a trading colony at *La Navidad*; determine whether he had found Marco Polo's land of Cipangu.

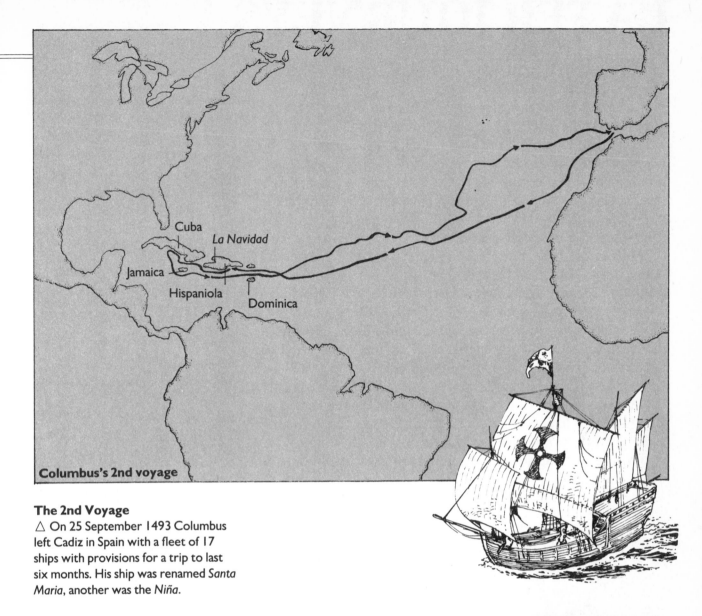

Columbus's 2nd voyage

Cuba
La Navidad
Jamaica
Hispaniola
Dominica

The 2nd Voyage
△ On 25 September 1493 Columbus
left Cadiz in Spain with a fleet of 17
ships with provisions for a trip to last
six months. His ship was renamed *Santa
Maria*, another was the *Niña*.

to his crew. Columbus spent some time exploring Dominica and
the group of islands, now known as The Windwards. Columbus
then sailed away to Hispaniola and the peace of *La Navidad*. It
was not to be! On reaching *La Navidad* he discovered that only
the walls of the fort were left. Whilst he had been away, a war
had broken out between rival groups of natives and the Spanish
settlers had joined in. They had all been massacred. The local
natives were still friendly, so Columbus tried again and
established a new outpost which he also called *Isabella*.

Leaving Pedro Margarit in command, Columbus set off again
to find China. He explored along the coast of Cuba for many
weeks but of course didn't reach China. On returning to
Isabella, Columbus was met by more disasters. Disease and war
had broken out. Not only that, but many of the settlers had
grown tired of Columbus's rules, which seemed designed only to
increase his own wealth and status. What was even worse was
that some had set sail back to Spain to complain about him. In
the spring of 1496 Columbus decided to return too – to defend
himself in front of Ferdinand and Isabella.

Timechart
The Indies were sighted on **3
November**. Guadeloupe was
reached seven days later.
Sailed on to *La Navidad* on
26 November.
New colony established at *Isabella*
on **2 January 1494**.
Searched for gold to centre of
Hispaniola in **March**.
Set sail for Cuba on **24 April 1494**.
During the next five months he
explored most of the coast of
Jamaica.
In **1495** Columbus tried to establish
peace and order on Hispaniola.
Sailed back to Spain on **10 March
1496**.

LATER JOURNEYS

Despite the relative failure of the second voyage, Columbus found he was still in favour with the King and Queen, and they were anxious for him to go on a third journey to the East. Ferdinand and Isabella were keen to gain as much land as possible for Spain and achieve superiority over Portugal. They also wanted to make sure that Hispaniola could be rescued as a trading station. Because of this they gave a pardon to hundreds of prisoners and paid for many other settlers to go to Hispaniola. Two ships, one of which was the *Niña*, set off with men and supplies in late 1497. Four months later Columbus also set off, with a fleet of six ships. He was to be a governor again. He wanted to convert the natives to Christianity and use them as workers on farms he would establish.

After being becalmed on the journey in the Doldrums for many days, Columbus vowed that the first land he saw would be named after The Holy Trinity, to thank God for their safe arrival. The island he landed on is still called Trinidad. The next day he sighted what he thought was an island that he named Isla Sancta – Holy Island. What he didn't realise was that he had sighted a tiny part of the huge land mass of South America. Believing he was on an island he never ventured inland.

Columbus's 3rd Voyage

December 1497/January 1498 men and supplies leave for Hispaniola.
May 1498 Columbus leaves for the 'East'.
13 July Columbus becomes becalmed in the 'Doldrums'.
22 July he sighted Trinidad.
August 1498 Columbus reached Hispaniola.
In the spring of 1500 Franscisco Bobadilla reaches Hispaniola to restore law and order.
October 1500 Columbus is arrested and sent home in chains.
17 December Columbus is released from prison.

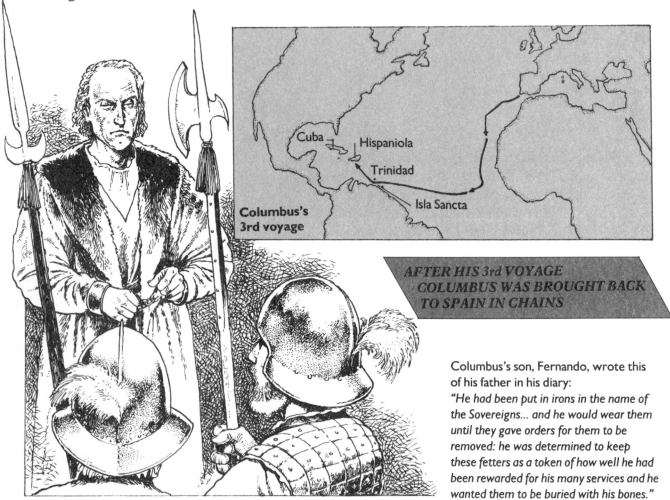

Cuba
Hispaniola
Trinidad
Isla Sancta
Columbus's 3rd voyage

AFTER HIS 3rd VOYAGE COLUMBUS WAS BROUGHT BACK TO SPAIN IN CHAINS

Columbus's son, Fernando, wrote this of his father in his diary:
"He had been put in irons in the name of the Sovereigns... and he would wear them until they gave orders for them to be removed: he was determined to keep these fetters as a token of how well he had been rewarded for his many services and he wanted them to be buried with his bones."

Columbus's 4th Voyage

May 1502 sailed from Spain. The crossing from the Canaries took 21 days. He landed in Martinique.
October 1502 the fleet anchored at Albureme.
The coast of Veragua (Panama) was reached on **6 January 1503**. Built a new settlement here in order to find gold.
Columbus had many problems, including being marooned on the island, that led to a mutiny on **2 January 1504**. Help was received from Spain and the rebellion was put down.
June 1504 a caravel arrived from Jamaica which took Columbus back to Santo Domingo.
Columbus arrives back in Spain on **7 November 1504.**

Columbus's house at Valladolid

Just one more trip

Although some of the men he had taken out with him were only interested in making a quick profit, many helped Columbus establish order and control. After two years Columbus sent a message back to Spain asking for other administrators to help him to run the country. The only man appointed was Francisco de Bobadilla. He almost instantly fell out with Columbus whom he disliked and mistrusted. Having been given powers by Ferdinand and Isabella to arrest corrupt officials and send them back to Spain, Bobadilla immediately arrested Columbus! He was put in irons on a ship back to Spain.

The King and Queen were easily persuaded to release Columbus. They even sacked Bobadilla. But it was obvious to Columbus that the sovereigns' attitude to him had changed. They were kind and grateful to him for all he had achieved but he was not made governor again. However, he was extremely wealthy and he was able to set off on yet another journey in 1502. This time he discovered and explored all along the coast of central America (Panama and Ecuador today). Although he still maintained that he had reached Asia, he had to admit that he had not found the way to China and Japan.

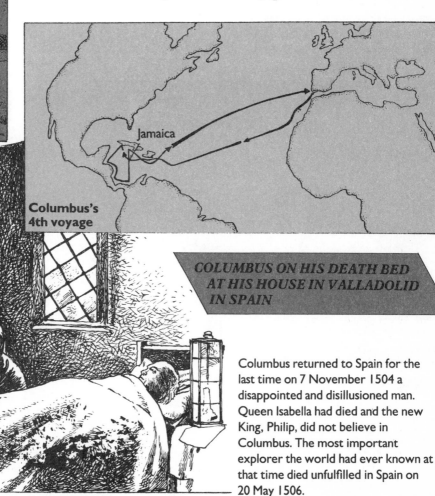

Jamaica

Columbus's 4th voyage

COLUMBUS ON HIS DEATH BED AT HIS HOUSE IN VALLADOLID IN SPAIN

Columbus returned to Spain for the last time on 7 November 1504 a disappointed and disillusioned man. Queen Isabella had died and the new King, Philip, did not believe in Columbus. The most important explorer the world had ever known at that time died unfulfilled in Spain on 20 May 1506.

THE NEW WORLD

After Columbus the world seemed to shrink. Explorers were inspired to go further. Perhaps as important was the fact that now others were prepared to put up the money to enable such voyages to happen.

In 1499-1500 the Portuguese navigator Amerigo Vespucci followed in the wake of Columbus and explored the South American coast down to the mouth of the Amazon River. The whole of this previously unnamed continent in the 'New World' was named America after him.

Between 1497 and 1499 Vasco da Gama followed the route of Bartholomew Diaz (see pages 8 and 9) round the Cape of Good Hope to explore the Indian Ocean. In 1498 he landed in India. In 1497 John Cabot became the first European to cross the Atlantic to sail to North America since the Vikings, 500 years before. He explored, and named, Newfoundland, as well as other parts of Canada.

Cortes

When Cortes landed in South America the native population was about 57 million. In less than 100 years this had dropped to just over 4 million. This was partly due to the wars that were fought. Most deaths, however, were because of the introduction of European diseases such as measles, smallpox and chickenpox, to which the natives had no immunity.

Eric Williams, who wrote a history of the Caribbean called *From Columbus to Castro* (the President of Cuba), said: "*Columbus's voyage was the first gold rush in the history of the modern world.*"

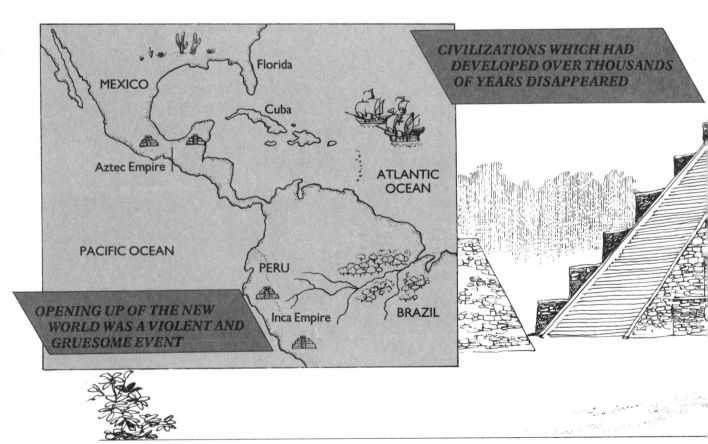

CIVILIZATIONS WHICH HAD DEVELOPED OVER THOUSANDS OF YEARS DISAPPEARED

OPENING UP OF THE NEW WORLD WAS A VIOLENT AND GRUESOME EVENT

Pizarro

The Spanish conquest of South America was completed by two explorers. Hernan Cortes overthrew the mighty Aztec Empire (in present-day Mexico), between 1519 and 1521. Francisco Pizarro, discovered and conquered the Inca Empire in Peru, between 1532 and 1534. Both brought back vast amounts of gold and silver.

The Treaty of Tordesillas had not been agreed to by other nations. They could not see any reason why the Spanish and the Portuguese should carve up the newly discovered world between them. This led to an illegal trade between Spain and other countries. The Spanish navy was supposed to sink any boat refusing to pay taxes to Spain for their trade. This led to the colourful and exciting raiding-party adventures of the English navigators Sir Francis Drake and John Hawkins.

Round the 'Horn' – and the world

The greatest explorer of all to follow in Columbus's path was Ferdinand Magellan. Just like Columbus he tried to get money from the Portuguese, and failed. Again he went on to the Spaniards, who put up the money for five ships, which set sail – to the west to reach the east! After just over a year, Magellan took his boats round Cape Horn at the southern tip of South America and into the Pacific Ocean. The Magellan Straits are still known by his name today. The following year, he reached the Pacific Islands which he christened the Philippines, after the King of Spain. Magellan was killed by natives in the Philippines, but his second-in-command, Juan Sebastian del Cano, continued the voyage and reached home, in Spain, in 1522. By following Columbus's vision, people had sailed round the world for the first time.

THE JOURNEY TODAY

We can be absolutely sure that Christopher Columbus travelled across to America so slowly he never needed to worry about jet-lag! How would he have coped with the idea that today it is possible to get into Concorde and travel so fast that you can arrive in a country thousands of kilometres away earlier than when you set off. Travelling to and from America is an unremarkable occurrence today for Europeans. But the development of long distance transport was slow.

It was the need to trade in the basic commodities that Columbus and other explorers discovered that forced the pace of change. For instance, in the 19th-century London tea merchants would wait at port for their sailing ships to arrive and whoever was first could charge for their goods whatever price they liked. So ships were made to go faster and faster. Some were so fast that they were called 'clippers' because of the way they clipped along across the open seas.

Record-breakers

There have been many different journeys across the Atlantic in the last 500 years:
In 1987 Tom McClain in his rowing boat took 54 days and 18 hours.
In 1936 the Liner *Queen Mary* took 4 days 27 minutes.
The first balloon crossing of the Atlantic was by three Americans in 1978. They took 6 days. Concorde regularly takes about 4 hours.

The biggest ship in the world, the oil tanker *Seawise Giant*, looks as though it might stretch most of the way across the Atlantic on its own! It is almost 500m long and weighs more than 500,000 tonnes. The *Santa Maria* was only 25m long. You could line up twenty of Columbus's flagship and still only make one *Seawise Giant*.

FASTEST CROSSING

The fastest Atlantic crossing was in 1974 by two majors of the United States Airforce. The average speed in their Lockheed SR-71A was just over 2908 km/h. The journey from New York to London took just 1 hr. 54 mins. 56.4 secs.

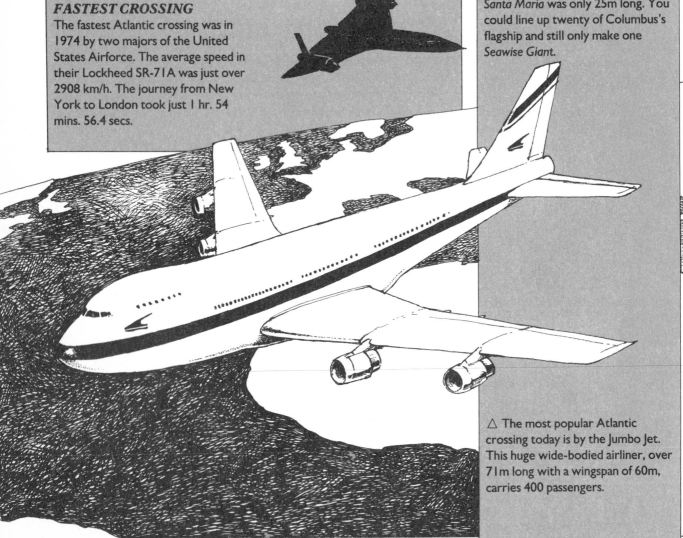

△ The most popular Atlantic crossing today is by the Jumbo Jet. This huge wide-bodied airliner, over 71m long with a wingspan of 60m, carries 400 passengers.

At the beginning of the 19th century, cargo ships laden with wool from Australia, minerals from South America, wheat from North America and coal from Europe, still had to go round the Cape of Good Hope at the southern tip of Africa to reach their destinations. Then in 1869 the Suez Canal was opened. Columbus would have been green with envy. To reach the East from Spain so easily! The Suez Canal meant that bigger cargo steamers could compete in speed with the clippers, and carry more cargo. The days of sail were largely over.

Cargo ships today carry sealed containers filled at a factory and lifted on board by a crane at the dockside. Ships carrying perishable goods such as fruit and meat are huge refrigerators. No need for live sheep and chickens for the crew to eat!

Modern navigational aids such as lightships, radio, radar and satellites have increased safety at sea. Special satellites such as Inmarsat and Navstar link thousands of ocean-going ships. Developments in radar mean that the location, speed and course of other ships is available to all captains. But one wonders if modern captains are as good as Columbus at dead-reckoning?

Perhaps the most unusual occurrence in the last few years is fitting modern ships with wing-sails, which work more like aircraft wings than old sails did. However, they push the ships forward rather than up. Everyone is trying hard to preserve fuel, and ships fitted with wing-sails can save up to 30 per cent in fuel costs. Perhaps Columbus would have enjoyed going by boat to America today after all!

Legacy of America

The following is a list of some of the goods brought back from the Americas to Europe by Columbus and other 15th- and 16th-century explorers:
Foods: Potatoes, beans, maize, cassava.
Medicines: Quinine, coca, strychnine.
Other items: Tobacco, large amounts of gold, American Indian, Aztec and Inca arts and crafts. Among these were silver statues of animals such as the llama, as above, which was previously unknown to Europeans.

FACTS AND FIGURES

SUMMARY OF COLUMBUS'S VOYAGES

August 1492 left Palos on first journey. Reached America on 12 October. Probably landed on Watling Island – now San Salvador. Also discovered Cuba and Haiti.

Returned to Spain in March 1493 when he was greatly honoured.
Second voyage between 1493-1496 on which he discovered the islands of Guadeloupe, Montserrat, Antigua, Porto Rico and Jamaica.

During the third voyage in 1498 he discovered Trinidad and the mainland of South America (although he didn't realise it).
Failed to colonise the island successfully and was sent back to Spain in chains in 1500.

During last voyage between 1502 and 1504 he explored the coast of Honduras and Nicaragua.
Died in 1506 sad and in relative poverty in Valladolid – buried in Seville cathedral.

COLUMBUS

Born in Genoa in Italy in 1451, he settled in Portugal in 1478. During his childhood he learned that he wanted to be a sailor, and dreamt of sailing west to reach the East. His ambition became an obsession. As much as he desired success for discovery itself, he wanted wealth and honours more. After a great deal of trying, in the end it was King Ferdinand and Queen Isabella of Spain who financed his first journey to 'America' in 1492. In the USA, Columbus Day – 12 October – is still a public holiday.

CORTES

He began his military campaign in 1519, when he and his 508 followers landed in Mexico. By 1521 he had succeeded in overthrowing the Aztecs. The main reasons for his success despite his very small number of troops was his diplomacy – and his possession of firearms and horses. In 1524 he led an arduous and pointless expedition to Honduras. After this Cortes spent most of his time in Mexico, but returned to Spain for the final years of his life.

PIZARRO

After making several scouting expeditions from Panama, Pizarro began his campaign of conquest in 1530 when he landed in Peru with with about 180 followers. Success came quickly after he had captured the Inca's ruler, Atahualpa, in 1532. He looted the Inca capital, Cuzco, in 1533 and had conquered the whole empire by 1535. However, he ruled very badly and some of his own men assassinated him in 1541.

GLOSSARY

ACCOLADE – a high award or prize usually given in public by a king or queen.

ASTROLABE – an instrument for measuring the heights of the Sun and the stars above the horizon.

AZORES – a group of nine islands in the North Atlantic.

BECALMED – when a sailing ship stays still at sea because the weather is without wind.

CAPE OF GOOD HOPE – The southern tip of South Africa, formerly named the Cape of Storms.

CANARIES – a group of volcanic islands 100km off the north-west coast of Africa which belong to Spain.

COMMISSION – a group of people appointed to carry out a certain task.

CONQUISTADORES – Spanish explorers and adventurers who went to sea to make their fortune.

DOLDRUMS – an area near the equator where there is little or no wind.

FLAGSHIP – the leading ship in a convoy, usually the Admiral's.

HOLY TRINITY – the idea that God exists as the Father, the Son and the Holy Spirit.

HOUR-GLASS – a closed glass tube made narrower in the middle like a figure 8 so that the sand inside can run from the top half to the bottom in half an hour.

LATITUDE – the position on a map measured as the distance to the North or South of the equator.

LEAGUE – an old measurement of length usually about 3 miles (4.8km). Columbus thought it was 4 miles (6.4km).

LOG – the daily record of a voyage or flight kept by the captain.

MUTINY – a sailors' revolt against their ship's captain.

PEN-PORTRAIT – a vivid written description of someone.

PLUMBLINE – a long line with a metal weight tied to it which was dropped over the side of a ship to measure the depth of the water in which it was sailing.

RUDDER CABLE – a length of thick rope that controlled the rudder and which was used to steer the ship.

SPAR – pole from which a sail is hung.

TRINKET – a small, fancy, inexpensive ornament like a bracelet or a ring.

INDEX